# 50 DRAG QUEENS

# QUEENS

## WHO CHANGED THE WORLD

# 50 DRAG QUEENS

## WHO CHANGED THE WORLD

A celebration of the most influential
drag artists of all time

**Dan Jones**

Hardie Grant

B O O K S

# Contents

# INTRODUCTION

Meet 50 of the most sickening drag queens ever to strut the world's catwalks, clubs and dive bars with nothing but a smear of glitter, a strip of duct tape and a pair of size 14 heels. Discover Princess Seraphina and the Midnight Masquerades of long-ago London, the legendary house mothers of the 1980s New York City drag scene, the contemporary Insta-famous superstars of *RuPaul's Drag Race* and many, many more. Here are the pioneers, mavericks and megastars of the international performance scene with all the charisma, uniqueness, nerve and talent needed to help shape the world of drag.

Drag is a deliciously queer-edged artform. Think of it at the centre of a glittery Venn diagram that can encompass theatre, comedy and political dissent with eroticism, fantasy, gender play and eye-poppingly voluminous wigs. Drag can happen anywhere, in any form, from bawdy jokes and lipsynched Britney hits in late-night bars, to dazzling art projects in upscale galleries or slick award-winning TV shows and video works that are taking over the digital space. And, for some, it's a clever disguise that allows unabashed queerness to exist even in the most oppressive of regimes.

What sets these 50 drag queens apart is a true dedication to their art, the bravery to do something different; disruptive – even dangerous. Together, they celebrate love, push boundaries, explore queerness, gender and identity and shine bright in a world where being fabulous and fierce is an act of resistance.

7

# RUPAUL

'If you can't love yourself, how the hell are you gonna love somebody else?' asks the bewigged RuPaul (born 1960), the iconic, larger-than-life ex-punk cover girl, and shrewd owner of a media empire. The world's most famous drag queen is a steely, often hilarious creation who only dresses up when the price is right.

Growing up in San Diego, RuPaul Charles struggled with being different. The age of 14 was a particularly dark time, as Ru thought 'I can't be the way society wants me to be,' but with the support of family, Ru knew his tribe was out there. A year later he moved with his sister to Atlanta, Georgia, to study performing arts. There, he found himself submerged in the underground cinema and punk music scene (with a little dancing on the side). But it was in the mid-80s that he moved from Atlanta to New York, stepped his impossibly long legs into a frock and became a superstar. You can spot him in the B-52s' 'Love Shack' video (1989), and soon he had his own pop mega hit with 'Supermodel (You Better Work)' (1992). Later, he hosted a chat show, performed a duet with Elton, hung out with Kurt Cobain and Courtney Love and became the first male face of MAC Cosmetics.

In 2009, after a period of relative career silence, he debuted *RuPaul's Drag Race*, then a low-budget TV commission that mocked the format of model reality shows. In it, fledgling drag queens compete for the top spot in a sequin-studded bun fight that makes for compulsive viewing. The not-so-secret subtext of the show is to reveal the lives of the men and trans women who take part in it, many of whom have been kicked out of home or struggle to make ends meet. The series won an Emmy in 2016.

RuPaul continues to be busy, launching a makeup line, recording albums and teaching America the filthiest drag slang imaginable. 'You Better Work' is a slogan to live by, it seems. So, to what does he owe his success? 'Kindness only goes so far,' says Ru, 'and then it's time to show your claws.'

'Kindness only goes so far
and then it's time to show your claws.'

# CONCHITA WURST

Conchita Wurst is the bearded beauty who defied the haters and united Europe through the power of a smoky eye, a simple French mani and a yearning to sing. Her Bond theme-inspired song, 'Rise Like a Phoenix', won the 2014 Eurovision Song Contest against a backdrop of homophobia, misogyny and populist politics – and it was truly wonderful.

In the run-up to the live televised contest (that attracts a staggering 183 million international viewers), Conchita's very existence – a flawless femme drag creation with a beard – became a hugely divisive issue. Across the world, cultural commentators and politicians felt the need to weigh in; some dazzled by her glamour, others disgusted with her queerness. Conservative groups, particularly in eastern Europe, found themselves with their knickers in a twist. Petitions to broadcasters in Belarus and Russia demanded Conchita be edited out of the show, and Russian politician Vitaly Milonov found Conchita's inclusion in the event 'homosexual propaganda', and the contest itself a 'hotbed of sodomy' marking the 'spiritual decay' of Europe. As the date of the final grew closer, the hate grew louder and louder.

Conchita is the alter-ego of Thomas Neuwirth (born 1988), the Austrian performer and TV talent show finalist. Neuwirth grew up in a small community in the mountains of Austria and faced prejudice for being gay, noting many gay people have had a similar experience. He first debuted his drag creation in 2011 and, by the time of the Eurovision final, voting for Conchita had become a vote against homophobia and small-mindedness – a vote in which anything could happen. On the night, she shone out with a stripped down, power-punch of a performance; a *tour de force* that secured her a win. With millions of Europeans of all creeds voting for Conchita, a little bit of history was made that night.

'Rise like a phoenix.'

# PRINCESS SERAPHINA

Now to Georgian London, and a city balls-deep in a binge-drinking crisis. In the 1720s, booze and vice were on tap in grimy taverns, squalid drinking rooms and brothels. Mother Clap's was the most infamous 'molly house', and the city's sauciest queer drinking venue. Against this backdrop, Princess Seraphina – perhaps England's first drag queen – stole the spotlight.

Through court transcripts and confessions, historian Rictor Norton has pieced together the story of the Princess, aka John Cooper, a star of the city's Midnight Masquerades. In these weekly carnivals, party-goers would wear a disguise: men would dress up as witches, nursemaids or shepherdesses; women would transform into sailors and hussars, and all manner of gender-bending naughtiness was had. Cooper would attend masquerades and parties as Princess Seraphina, her signature look: a white gown and racy scarlet cloak, with a fan to flutter at fine gentlemen.

Norton believes the Princess was an integral part of John Cooper's identity. In July 1732, he prosecuted another man, Thomas Gordon, for stealing his clothes during a mysterious scuffle in the bushes. Gordon was acquitted, but it's these court documents that reveal the startling life of the Princess in deliciously gossipy detail. Everyone from the local barmaid, stocking maker and washerwoman had an eyebrow-raising to say about 'her Highness', who had something of a local reputation. There was a sense of defiance and bravery about Cooper; Princess Seraphina allowed him to cross the gender lines, meet men and become the neighbourhood bad girl in a time when male same-sex attraction was completely taboo. Flutter your fan at that.

**Princess Seraphina
stole the spotlight.**

# DORIAN
# COREY

'I always had hopes of being a big star. But as you get older, you aim a little lower,' says Dorian Corey (1937–1993) in cult documentary *Paris is Burning* (1990). 'Everybody wants to make an impression, some mark upon the world. Then you think, you've made a mark on the world if you just get through it, and a few people remember your name. Then you've left a mark.'

Dorian Corey was a drag artist, mind-blowing fashion and costume designer and *bon vivant* who loved the creativity, fun and fame of performing. Originally from Buffalo, New York, in the late 1950s, Corey was a window dresser for a department store before moving to New York City to study at Parsons School of Design by day and dance in a saucy snake-powered dance review at night with a boa constrictor.

In the 1970s, the young trans woman became a face on the ballroom scene, even running her own house, but it was her costume design that set her apart from the other house mothers. Her looks were legendary: the sequins, the headdresses and, not least, a giant feather cape that would unfurl and cover half the audience. And, of course, Corey ended up in Jennie Livingston's *Paris* documentary.

Although some of her posthumous fame has been a little tricky to navigate (after her death in 1993, the less said about what those clearing out Corey's wardrobe discovered, the better), there's no doubt that Corey was a legend. She was a woman who made her mark.

Costume design set her apart
from the other mothers.

# CARLOTTA

Carlotta is the stage name of Carol Spencer (born 1943), the legendary Australian cabaret artist and one-time member of Les Girls, an infamous 1960s drag review in Kings Cross, Sydney, where Carlotta was star and host for decades. In the 60s and 70s, Les Girls was the jewel in Sydney's late night clubland, a must-see for visiting celebs like Liza Minnelli, Frank Sinatra and Shirley Bassey, and Carlotta and the girls became known for their showgirl glamour and saucy numbers.

Carlotta's influence on Australian pop-culture is huge: she's an ex-soap opera actor, the inspiration behind Terrence Stamp's character Bernadette in *The Adventures of Priscilla, Queen of the Desert* (1994), a TV panellist and chat show guest, and *Carlotta* (2014), the ABC TV movie of her life, told the true story of Spencer's life to mainstream audiences.

In Australia, there's a lot of love for Carlotta and the memory of Les Girls (there's even a portrait of Carlotta in the National Portrait Gallery in Canberra), but Spencer is often keen to point out how controversial the act was in its heyday: its blurring of gender boundaries, the mix of men and trans women in the line-up; in many ways it was startlingly modern. As a transgender woman herself, Carol has been the go-to expert on trans issues on Australian TV for decades, holding the nation's hand as it grappled with new ideas about gender. All hail the queen of the Cross.

**All hail the queen
of the Cross.**

# VENUS DIMILO

Imagine if 'a punk had sex with a clown,' says British drag queen Sophie Harris (born 1991), 'and that baby got adopted by someone who knew how to dress really well in the 80s/90s. That's Venus Dimilo.'

Sophie fell in love with drag at a club night celebrating cult documentary *Paris is Burning*. She wore a cheap wig and a paper neck ruffle made from magazine pages: 'It wasn't really drag, but I made an effort!' At first, she found the other performers fierce and intimidating, but Sophie and her friends won trophies, danced and an idea started to form. 'I felt so special to be in that inner circle'. She knew there and then she wanted to perform.

Venus Dimilo, Sophie's drag creation, has a leftfield, 90s-edge in bodysuits, leather or custom gowns. Her performance influences are varied, from feminism, the planets and retro film to 80s pop band Bananarama, Angela Lansbury (her true love), her drag sisters and her own body: Sophie has TAR syndrome. 'I love using my arms as part of a performance, or joking about it,' she explains. 'It's not my entire identity but it's a big part of me. Disability is viewed as a negative and I want to teach people to look at it in a different light. That could be by educating someone or showing others they can do anything they want. I'm the drag queen with no arms and I love it; there's no point in hiding it away.'

There might be a lack of diversity in drag, but that's changing, says Sophie. 'AFAB [assigned female at birth] queens are becoming more commonplace,' she explains, 'but AFAB people are still a minority on the gay scene, as are trans people. We all have struggles that need bringing to people's attention. Drag is a great platform to show that and raise awareness.'

**'I'm the drag queen with
no arms and I love it.'**

# JINKX MONSOON

Jinkx Monsoon (born 1987) has always done it her own way. Her vintage-edged, intellectual and topsy turvy charm school drag style was somewhat at odds with her fellow contestants on *Drag Race 5*. But her eerily accurate impression of 'Little Edie' Bouvier Beale from *Grey Gardens*, a performance that in turn delighted and confused the other queens (some had no idea quite who 'Little Edie' was), made her stand out, and she was the surprise winner of the season.

One million Instagram followers later, Jinkx has become an international cabaret star, touring with productions like *Drag Becomes Her* (2018), *Hocum Pokem* (2019) or her ongoing *Vaudevillains* collaboration with fellow performer Major Scales. It makes sense that Jinkx's creator, Seattle-born Jerick Hoffer, is a theatre graduate, and is just as at home playing characters like Velma Von Tussell in *Hairspray* or a cabaret club owner in CBS's *Blue Bloods* than their own self-penned shows.

*Drag Race* fame hasn't changed Jinkx's off-beat style and she loves to play small venues, to sings songs, chat and tell jokes, much like the old-time idols that inspire her. She still does things her own way: now and again, she wrong-foots her fans with something wonderfully unexpected. Name another queen who has covered Radiohead's *Creep*, transforming it into a creepy *Josie & the Pussycats*-style torch song. Well played, Jinkx Monsoon, well played.

**Well played, Jinkx Monsoon, well played.**

# LADY BUNNY

All hail Lady Bunny (born 1962), the drag queen's drag queen. Her voluminous, bouffant-style blonde wig and short shift dresses plant her style firmly in the 1960s, with all the appropriately un-PC jokes and political side-swipes to boot. She's whip-smart, deliciously spiky and proudly old school, still flying the flag for the angry, reactionary and truly subversive drag of the 1980s and 90s.

Bunny is a contemporary of RuPaul (page 8), an ex-club kid and organiser of legendary drag event Wigstock. She's the queen of the New York City drag scene but grew up as Jon Ingle in Tennessee and, after a year in Ghana, remembers sneaking into a club in Chattanooga aged 13 to see drag veteran Tasha Khan, and was subsequently romanced by the sequins, glamour and Khan's incredible stage presence. Her parents sent her to a boarding school in the UK to straighten her out, but she moved back two years later, no straighter, and with an even more rounded world view. She met RuPaul Charles at college in Atlanta and was again romanced by the drag scene. The pair became go-go dancers and moved to New York City together in 1983, and the rest is history.

Since those early New York City days, RuPaul and Lady Bunny's paths may have differed, but they've both achieved eye watering success: RuPaul as an international media mogul, and Lady Bunny as a legendary, cult performer and drag inspiration, loved and feared by all.

**She's whip-smart, deliciously spiky
and proudly old school.**

# BOB THE DRAG QUEEN

There's a whiff of Vaginal Davis (page 46) about Bob the Drag Queen, whose performance style feels close to Davis' anti-drag drag, at odds with the hyper-real, hyped-up glamour of mainstream queenery. But it was those mainstream queens from *Drag Race* who first inspired Bob to get into her first pair of heels, and her level-headed, confident and comedic drag scored her the top spot in season eight. Since then, Bob has created a startling performance career with sell-out live shows of her podcast *Sibling Rivalry* with Monét X Change *and* acting in Vimeo/HBO's *High Maintenance* and Netflix's *Tales of the City*, plus Berkeley Rep's *Angels in America*.

Bob is the alter-ego of comic Caldwell Tidicue (born 1986), the Georgia-born New Yorker and slam poet who, pre-*Drag Race*, had built up quite the fanbase in New York City through comedy performances and activist antics: in 2001, Bob began staging weekly wedding ceremonies with her drag sisters in Times Square, protesting for LGBTQ+ equality.

**A startling performance career
with sell-out live shows.**

# DAME EDNA EVERAGE

Hello Possums! In the late 1950s, she was just a dowdy, buttoned-up 'average Australian housewife' from Moonee Ponds, Melbourne, but decades later Dame Edna Everage is transformed into a glamorous self-described international mega star. With a pair of sparkling harlequin glasses and a pale lilac blush wig, Everage is truly iconic, with one foot in drag, the other in mainstream entertainment, and the world in between.

Edna is the drag alter-ego of comedian, actor and author Barry Humphries (born 1934). Inspired by the sweetly humdrum Country Women's Association, Humphries first debuted uptight Edna on stage in 1955, and re-worked her until she truly found her groove in the 1980s when Humphries gave the character a Thatcher-like edge.

As her popularity grew she scored film and TV roles, successful theatre shows around the world and TV specials, particularly in the UK. One of her chat shows, ITV's *The Dame Edna Experience*, saw big ticket celebs like Charlton Heston, Lauren Bacall and Germaine Greer line up to be humiliated, adored or dropped through a trap door.

In the UK and US, this Dame is a household name, but in Australia, Everage and Humphries are considered true icons. Although honoured with a postage stamp, a street name and statue, it's perhaps Edna's slow-burn comedy that she'll be remembered for. Her trademark long, polite preamble to a punchline – usually a perfectly-observed put-down – is like waiting for a bomb to drop.

**One foot in drag, the other
in mainstream entertainment.**

# FALUDA ISLAM

Multi-disciplinary artist Zulfi Ali Bhutto (born 1990) explores with the intersection of Islam, sexuality and masculinity via monobrowed drag beauty, Faluda Islam.

Zulfi first used visual and performance works to explore Islamic and queer identity after coming to study at the San Francisco Art Institute in 2014. Heir to a political dynasty in Pakistan, violence has been a constant in Zulfi's life: his father was killed outside his home in Karachi, his grandfather was assassinated in a military coup, and his uncle and aunt were murdered. He was shocked by the anti-Muslim sentiment in everyday American life, and truly shaken by the Pulse massacre in 2016. He had to do something. With the help of fellow creative Ana Montenegro, Faluda was created as a response to these ideas and events; a sparkling, politically savvy drag character, timeless and multi-national, just a girl who wants to challenge misconceptions, blur boundaries and have fun.

Although based in San Francisco, Zulfi's career is of interest to a feverish South Asian media but – for a short time – the artist enjoyed a brief spell under the radar in the US. When a video of Zulfi's joyous drag creation was posted on the internet in 2017, it found its way to anti-queer Pakistani media and right-wing political commentators (they were not happy). Zulfi continues to develop his art, through 'Prayformances' (praying with a female partner in public spaces in the US), and gorgeous textile pieces that explore the idea of the 'strong Muslim man', Faluda continues to dance and spin, proof that queer Muslims exist – and they're 100 per cent here to party.

**Faluda continues to
dance and spin.**

# BIANCA DEL RIO

Like the potty-mouthed variety hosts of old, superstar drag queen comedian Bianca Del Rio describes herself as an insult-comic, shooting out fiery one-liners and put-downs that floor her fans – and they love her for it. Arguably the most famous of all the *Drag Race* queens (she won *Drag Race 6*, the first Latinx performer to do so), the world-weary gravel-voiced quip-machine is known for her trademark cartoonish hyper-drag makeup, love of sparkles, and – with a successful stage career with stints in *Rent, Cabaret* and *Everyone's Talking About Jamie* – she's fast becoming a household name.

Del Rio is the creation of Roy Haylock (born 1975), a costumier and designer of Cuban and Honduran descent, via Louisiana; Haylock is now based firmly in New York City. A one-time costume designer for the New Orleans Opera, Haylock first appeared in drag in a performance of *Pageant* in 1996. He was noticed by fellow drag performer Lisa Beaumann who encouraged him to turn to the drag side. Bianca was born, and Haylock won New Orleans Gay Entertainer of the Year Award three years in a row (plus a slew of New Orleans Gay Bitch of the Year Award nominations, but who's counting?). Hurricane Katrina marked a turning point for Haylock: he had spent 10 years grafting, working in a bar five days a week and making costumes for theatre productions, with only modest success, and decided to move to New York City. In 2005 Bianca was thrust into the spotlight and she quickly started to pick up comedy awards and a loyal following.

Del Rio's success is astounding. There's the crowd-funded Netflix movie *Hurricane Bianca* (2016) and its follow-up *From Russia with Hate* (2018); sell-out international comedy tours, a self-help book and 2 million Instagram followers – anything less would be insulting.

**Arguably the most famous of
all the *Drag Race* queens.**

# RICKY RENÉE

In Bob Fosse's *Cabaret* (1972), young straight-laced Brian (Michael York) notices – with some surprise – a glamorous female presence standing next to him at the urinal. It's Elke, a performer and hostess at the infamous Kit Kat Klub in WWII Berlin, who returns his look with a smile. It's a delightfully understated gender-clash moment, and Fosse chose a truly artful drag performer to perfect it.

One-time child star Jack Renner (born 1929) loved the stage, but it was performing at the Jewel Box Club in his native Florida that his star truly started to shine. After a brief stint in the military, the all-singing, all-dancing performer joined the club's troupe of drag queens and, as Ricky Renée, soon out-performed the others, razzle-dazzling his way to headline the bill. Ricky was then a sensation in London's clubland (*Quick Change Artist*, a British Pathé film from 1967 features him headlining a London club in various male and female guises), before touring Europe and ending up on the big screen in *Cabaret*.

In his time, Ricky shared the stage with Ella Fitzgerald, Josephine Baker and even opened his own club, Ricky Renée's, in Soho, London, in the late 1960s. Like his own Hollywood crush – Marylin Monroe – Ricky Renée was a blonde bombshell who inspired many; Lady Bunny (page 22) cites Ricky as an influence for her own 60s-edged look. And, legend has it, one night at Ricky's Soho club Shirley Bassey was so enamoured with one of his looks (a beaded chiffon and silk number with endless feather boa) that she ordered an exact copy of it there and then.

**An inspirational blonde bombshell –
razzle-dazzling his way to headline.**

# DRAG SYNDROME

Meet Drag Syndrome, a collective of British drag artists with Down's syndrome who have taken the performance world by storm. Starring Lady Francesca, Horrora Shebang (award-winning film-maker and actor, Otto Baxter), Gaia Callas and drag king Justin Bond, the troupe have become known for their eye-poppingly energetic, visceral and joyful spirit – and a truckload of sass.

Drag Syndrome formed with the help of Culture Device, the British experimental dance company that works with exceptional artists who have DS. In the past few years, Culture Device and their artists have delivered 15 upscale projects from ballet to a dance residency at London's Royal Opera House. Drag was a new direction and it wasn't until that first underground performance in March 2018 that artistic director Daniel Vais realised quite how big the troupe was going to be.

From their first show, Drag Syndrome have scored rave reviews, feverish media attention – and more than its fair share of trolling from those who find the combination of queer-edged performance and people with DS too mind-blowing to comprehend. But, haters gonna hate and, with the troupe performing in venues around the world, appearing at legendary festivals such as Glastonbury, and enjoying the kind of packed tour schedule other artists can only dream of, it's definitely Drag Syndrome who are having the last laugh.

It's definitely Drag Syndrome
who are having the last laugh.

# LILY
# SAVAGE

The UK's finest drag queen comic, the award-winning Lily Savage was all endless twig-like legs, doorstop eyelashes, a mass of ash-blond curls (with regrowth) and a mouth like a sewer. It was in 1978 that Lily started her long strut from Merseyside to stardom, performing on small stages and pubs, building to an eight-year residency in London's revered Royal Vauxhall Tavern (the first building in the UK to gain special status because of its importance to the LGBTQ+ life). Although already popular in London and in gay clubs across the UK, it was Lily's Edinburgh Festival performances in the early 90s that made her a household name, scoring her TV presenting gigs and television stand-up specials. Not bad for a leggy gal from the Wirral.

Savage is – or rather was – the creation of Paul O'Grady (born 1955), the Irish-English comedian, performer, broadcaster, and gay- and animal-rights activist. The one-time working-class kid based Lily on different aspects of his female relatives, and first tried out the character in London before touring her in duos and reviews, allowing her no-nonsense, cynical AF personality and trademark death-stare to develop into a seamless, equally loved and feared persona in the British drag tradition. After decades of walking in Lily's shoes, O'Grady pulled the plug on the character in the mid-2000s and became a much-loved figure in his own right. Endless accolades, a loyal fanbase and an award from the Queen underline O'Grady's genius – and Lily's savage sense of humour.

**Not bad for a leggy gal from The Wirral.**

# THE COCKETTES

Glitter-encrusted queer performance group The Cockettes was drag on acid. Formed in 1969 from the infamous San Francisco commune scene (where more than 300 groups shared food, skills and undies), The Cockettes believed themselves to be the most creative, artistic and beautiful gang in the city – and then some. In a time of LSD-inspired, underground film, music, art and writing, The Cockettes found themselves at the epicentre of a cultural movement. Its members genuinely thought the world was on the brink of revolution – and it was in this atmosphere their most jaw-dropping work was performed.

The Cockettes' look, partly created by founder member, Hibiscus (aka George Edgerly Harris III), was artfully improvised with drag-edged glitter-beards, wonky eye-makeup and vintage tea dresses, marked them out as unique on the performance circuit.

As their fame grew, the group's original ethos – including performing for free – began to change. Hibiscus departed just before The Cockettes' much-feted 1971 trip to perform in New York City (where news crews reported on the curious incident of 47 passengers who had boarded a plane in full drag). The show was hottest ticket in town with John Lennon and Yoko Ono in the audience on opening night, along with Liza Minelli, Gore Vidal and Truman Capote. It was a wonderful disaster: The Cockettes' San Franciscan style didn't translate to New York City audiences. Legend has it that Angela Lansbury walked out, followed by Andy Warhol and his Factory friends, and reviews were woeful. The Cockettes' fame began to wane, but, with such a huge cast list, many of the group went on to have startling careers. Disco star Sylvester was a Cockette original, and Divine (page 70) guest-starred in notable performances. But, The Cockettes' legend lives on in every contemporary glitter-bearded alt-drag performer – and anyone who strives to be offbeat and do something truly radical.

**The hottest ticket in town.**

# DREAMTIME DIVAS

Meet the Dreamtime Divas, aka Nova Gina and Lasey Dunaman, the glittering drag performance duo from Kempsey, New South Wales. Both stars of Adrian Russell Will's feature doc *Black Divaz* (2018), Nova is the alter ego of Dunghutti man Dallas Webster, an Indigenous Australian, who debuted his creation in Sydney before returning to Kempsey and teaming up with his partner in crime TJ Hamilton (Lasey Dunaman) and creating Dreamtime Divas.

Growing up gay in a small town anywhere can be hard. TJ is a survivor of anti-gay violence, and Dallas found solace in Sydney as a teenager and lived there 20 years, but – somewhat unexpectedly – it's back in rural Australia that both performers have found love, acceptance and a successful entertainment career. TJ's Lasey Dunaman (a play on the name of Indigenous Australian singer Casey Donavan) and Nova first performed together in a local ex-servicemen's club to a hopped-up crowd unfamiliar with drag. They remember feeling nervous but it was a night that changed everything – they were a smash hit and, with support from Indigenous elders, the Dreamtime Divas have continued to be popular performers in rural New South Wales and beyond.

**It was a night that changed everything.**

# ALYSSA EDWARDS

Big wigs, limb-defying dance moves, signature tongue pops and a homely Texan drawl only bettered by Jerry Hall, Alyssa Edwards is one of the most influential performers in the modern drag world.

A serial drag-pageant winner (she's been picking up awards since 2004), Edwards is a seasoned performer, dancer and choreographer, and – as Justin Johnson (born 1980) – even runs her own award-winning dance studio in Mesquite, Texas, the subject of the Netflix show *Dancing Queen*.

Alyssa has strutted her stuff since the early 2000s, but the desire to perform was instilled much earlier, during Johnson's local little league games, where he was wowed by the pomp and fizz of the halftime shows. He was soon enrolled in dance classes but it wasn't until he was 19 that the small-town boy went to his first gay club and found himself mesmerised by a drag show. He entered an amateur drag contest soon after and thought up the name Alyssa (after Alyssa Milano) on the spot.

Appearing as a contestant on *Drag Race* in 2012 was a turning point for Edwards and, even though she wasn't particularly successful on the show, her influence is legendary. She now runs her own drag house, the Haus of Edwards, tours extensively, and juggles promo appearances and product collaborations with running the dance studio (her first love).

Edwards' antics have launched a thousand memes but she's been around long enough to remember pre-*Drag Race* when drag was an underground, hidden thing, at odds with the mainstream.

**Big wigs and
limb-defying dance moves.**

# JULIAN ELTINGE

The success of legendary (yet, with hindsight, rather tricky) drag performer and actor Julian Eltinge will have you snatching off your lace-front and flinging it in disgust. At one time in his career, Eltinge is thought to have been the world's highest paid actor. And they say drag doesn't pay the bills.

Born in Massachusetts in 1881, Eltinge was something of a child star before storming the stage as a vaudeville and Broadway performer, working his way up to incredible success. As a drag artist, Eltinge's didn't seek to make fun of gendered tropes, but to perform as a woman. In fact, in his earlier career, he was usually billed just as 'Eltinge', creating a mystery around his own gender. He was known to de-wig on stage, shocking the crowd, and toured internationally winning awards and eye-popping ticket sales. Silent film came next, then a career performing in Hollywood, and his own villa in LA – his Xanadu. As femme as he was on stage or screen, real life was another matter. Eltinge was known for his explosive anger, bar brawls and threats towards anyone who questioned his sexuality. (Dorothy Parker described him as 'ambisextrous'.)

Eltinge's drag career is awe-inspiring – but hard to love. In 1908 he joined a performance troupe and for two years, until 1910, Eltinge appeared on stage primarily in blackface: shocking by today's standards. Although this short period of Eltinge's career was years before the Jim Crow segregation laws were unpicked, and attitudes started to shift, he nevertheless benefitted from performing as a racist caricature. Can we still admire a drag queen's career knowing their past transgressions? Whatever you think of Eltinge, his mainstream success as a performer put drag on a whole new level.

**Drag on a whole new level.**

# VAGINAL DAVIS

Gender revolutionary Vaginal Davis (born 1969) doesn't fit neatly into any category – not even drag. The cultural firestarter is an award-winning performer and visual artist, painter, composer, zine- and film-maker, and founder of the infamous Bushwick drag community; Davis has always done things her own way.

From the LA underground performance scene of the late 1970s, Davis found herself at the centre of counter-cultural scenes, from homo-core punk to concept bands Black Fag and Afro Sisters, with her wonderfully topsy turvy lo-fi drag shows in Bushwick, New York a career high point. It was there Davis turned the art-form on its bewigged head. Flipping a chipped manicured middle finger to drag's pursuit of realness, flawless makeup, fake boobs and false eyelashes, Davis defiantly dragged up with just a little eye shadow, lipstick and wig, and set to the stage. It was particularly transgressive, her performance being somewhere between glamour and camp, with one queer theory academic calling it 'terrorist drag'. As her performance and art career grew, Davis shone brightly, becoming a muse to choreographer Pina Bausch and fashion designer Rik Owens – even David Bowie was a fan.

Today, Davis' work further explores gender, sexuality and race – specifically blackness and the blatino experience – using humour and insight to upset conservative thinking. Inspired by her revolutionary feminist and activist mother, it makes sense that her childhood crush was Angela Davis. It was a version of the Black Panther member she hoped to recreate with her Vaginal Davis moniker; a powerful, sexy revolutionary who says what others will not.

Davis has always done
things her own way.

# PANTI BLISS

Panti Bliss, the queen of Irish drag, knows what it's like to be put in her place. A controversy involving homophobia, Irish state broadcaster RTÉ – and a group of anti-equal marriage politicians, journalists and campaigners – saw her threatened with legal action. It also made her, as she has put it, 'an accidental gay rights activist'.

Pandora Panti Bliss is the glamorous creation of County Mayo's Rory O'Neill (born 1968), who debuted Panti in 1998, and is a stalwart on the gay Dublin scene, even running a gay venue in the city. Although much-loved by the queer community in Ireland, it was an interview on RTÉ in 2014 that brought Panti's talents to wider attention. As part of her campaign work for equal-marriage in Ireland, Panti said that, in her opinion, certain Irish anti-equal marriage journalists were homophobic. The journalists complained, and a speedy RTÉ apology ensued, then a hefty pay-out, a media blackout, and legal action against the channel and Rory himself.

Panti's fans and equal marriage advocates were horrified. At the height of the controversy, aka Pantigate, Panti delivered a speech at Abbey Theatre in Dublin; it was a blisteringly emotional, truly captivating monologue, with all the pain, anger and grace of a woman wronged. But then, some good news: Panti gained support from activists, politicians and celebs, and a referendum on the issue a year later saw equal marriage finally legalised in the Ireland. Panti Bliss is a queen making history.

'An accidental
gay rights activist.'

# CRÈME FATALE

San Francisco is a city that boasts the most inclusive drag community in the world, and is also home to the jewel-encrusted, pastel-toned confection known as Crème Fatale. Her artfully constructed 'chubby alien baby' look is extraordinary, her makeup skills otherworldly, and she has a 100K+ Instagram following that some of Mama Ru's girls would give all their veneers for.

Crème draws on 50s kitsch, 90s club kids (especially nightlife celeb Kabuki Starshine) and her own oddball sense of humour to create fantastical looks for performances in her own San Franciscan hood, Los Angeles and across the States – most notably at Sasha Velour's cult drag experience, *Nightgowns*. It all started in San Francisco when a young Fatale – *Crème fresh*, if you will – started to post pictures of her makeup transformations on Instagram. They drew the attention of some famous SF queens who invited her to drag night in the city and the rest is history.

In the San Franciscan drag scene it doesn't matter what gender you are (Crème is female), so, when online critics try to enforce a men's club mentality to the artform, it comes as a surprise – and an opportunity. She deftly turned one trolling comment, 'where's the transformation, sis?' into a merchandise line. There's a wider conversation about gender diversity in the drag world, and Crème is part of a growing community who remain positive about the incredible women who perform – and support drag – often in spaces some men feel are their own.

**Her 'chubby alien baby'
look is extraordinary.**

# THE VIVIENNE

Growing up, The Vivienne (aka James Lee Williams) was fascinated with makeup and its near-supernatural power to transform. Confident and out at school in Wales, Viv would turn up with a Louis Vuitton bag and Chanel glasses – until they were confiscated. 'It wasn't all bad, though,' she told *Vada Magazine*, 'I was stood outside the headmaster's office one day and another teacher walked past. She gave me a look up and down and told me I looked fabulous.'

At 16, she worked the beauty counter at a department store in Liverpool and started to cultivate her own drag look. Her first gig – door bitch at a local queer night – earned her £25, some booze and her drag name – inspired by her love of Vivienne Westwood. Drawing on the spirits of Cher and Bette Midler (Viv's *Hocus Pocus* look is something to behold), but with a Liverpool twist, Viv's star shines bright. She now performs internationally with RuPaul crowning her the UK's first Drag Race Ambassador and, in 2019, Viv went on to win the first ever season of *Drag Race UK*. (Her Snatch Game impression of Donald Trump has to be seen to be believed.)

Her look is inspired by the fun-loving, glamorous women of Liverpool (locals there are affectionately known as 'Scousers'), including the infamous Scouse Brow – the thick eyebrow look popular in the city. As one of Ru's girls, The Vivienne wants to be a true ambassador for the show, elevating drag to new heights and seeing it recognised as an artform where performance, comedy, after-dark weirdness and true transformation can happen.

**Inspired by the fun-loving glamorous women of Liverpool.**

# KUMAR

Through the sparkles and sass, drag has the power to bring queerness to mainstream audiences, but the performer's own sexuality is often hidden in plain sight. Drag comic Kumar, aka Kumarason Chinnadurai (born 1968), the Singapore-born Indian entertainer and actor, performed for more than two decades before deciding to break down the barrier between his on-stage and off-stage persona. Coming out as gay in 2011 was a radical move, especially in socially conservative Singapore where LGBTQ+ people have few rights. Today, he is one of the most well-known and best-loved comic performers of his generation – who just happens to be gay.

Known for his white-knuckle, politically-edged humour, Kumar came up through the Singapore cabaret club circuit and there is something of the old-style entertainer about him: his comic timing is whip-smart and his work ethic is astounding. Dealing in race, sex and everyday life in Singapore, Kumar's provocative act has come to the attention of the authorities – he has annually performed his routine for a police audience before being allowed to take his act public. But even this censorious approach hasn't dampened Kumar's fame: he's as popular as ever on stage and screen; a loved TV presenter and one-time sitcom actor star alongside Hong Kong megastar Carole Cheng. In 2011, he celebrated his career with a glossy biography by Ivan Lim, exploring his rise to fame via candid stories and a series of wonderfully camp photographic portraits, entitled *Kumar: From Rags to Drag*.

**Drag has the power to bring queerness to mainstream audiences.**

# HUNGRY

Hungry is a Berlin-based drag wunderkind and digital influencer whose artful creative projects flip traditional drag on its be-wigged head. Through meticulous makeup and costume, lines fracture and panel the face, eyes drop, stretching down the face, contact lenses obscure eyeballs, crusts of sparkles and studs of pearls are like odd growths; Hungry calls it 'distorted drag'.

Fashion design grad Hungry grew up in small town Bavaria and cites camp cult films *The Rocky Horror Picture Show* and *Party Monster* as early creative inspirations. When friends took them to a drag night in Berlin, Hungry felt inspired and, as time passed, their interest grew. Through their own designs and ideas and looks gifted from friends, Hungry's own unique aesthetic began to form. And then, following a move to London to intern at Aitor Throup and Vivienne Westwood, Hungry had a revelation. Drag didn't need to be beautiful or real, it could be artful, androgynous and, well, 100 per cent crazy.

Since focusing their creativity on drag, Hungry's career is booming; they painted and pearled-up Bjork for her Utopia imagery, they manage an incredible digital following (over 400K followers and counting) and perform internationally, mainly in queer venues. Imagine, through the dry ice and screams, Hungry appears – masked and trussed up in a corset and androgynous, alien-like garb, lipsynching to an ethereal Robyn remix – and the audience go from boozed-up clubgoers to gallery visitors, witness to something truly extraordinary.

**Distorted drag.**

# LYPSINKA

If lipsynching were an Olympic sport, John Epperson would be a multi-winning gold medallist. As Lypsinka, Epperson's drag persona, he has devoted himself to mastering a genre of stagecraft that requires surgical precision, a supremely geeky knowledge of vintage cinema, pop music and comedy, and impossibly flexible lips.

Epperson was born in 1955 in Mississippi; he trained as a classical pianist and worked for the American Ballet Theatre in New York City before drifting into his own brand of performance, debuting Lypsinka in the early 90s. Using his own audio know-how, Epperson creates intricate soundscapes using clips from old Hollywood movies and songs, lipsynching in perfect time. He's now a performance icon, known for devising verbatim theatre projects as well as writing his own lipsynch shows. Epperson is something of a cult figure, much loved by celebs, and often pops up in TV shows and movies. Darren Aronofsky cast Epperson in a minor role in *Black Swan* (2010) as a pianist for a dance company, its split-personality narrative resounding with Epperson.

Using clips, Epperson's act celebrates iconic female performers, letting them speak for themselves, and yet still retains his own unique character. In this way, he sidesteps the misogynistic banter that other male drag performers can fall into, creating something new, powerful and celebratory.

**Epperson is something
of a cult figure.**

# REGINA FONG

Please be upstanding for Her Imperial Highness, the Grand Duchess Regina Fong, a blood-red wigged member of the ill-fated Romanoffs who escaped the storming of the Winter Palace in 1917 St Petersburg only to end up in the UK under the protection of the British Royal family. Or so the legend goes.

Regina was the frizz-haired creation of Reg Bundy (born 1946), a British dancer, actor and cabaret performer who found fame as a 'West End Wendy' dancing in many shows in London's West End before unleashing Regina onto the world. Reg's drag creation was developed in infamous London venue The Black Cap where he performed alongside contemporaries and rivals such as Lily Savage and Dave Lynn. According to Paul O'Grady (Lily Savage, page 36), Regina Fong's ultra-regal character suited Bundy down to a tea, as he felt his time in the West End gave him a refined edge over other performers. His act – surreal, powered by pop culture references, jingles and audio from old movies – required perfectly timed audience participation. And Fong help you if you got it wrong.

Legendary writer, director and performer Neil Bartlett, a friend and collaborator of Reg, remembers a rather humble performer behind the regal exterior. '[He] never believed he was either especially beautiful or especially talented – but boy, could he inspire. Just to be in the same room as his ebullient, glamorous nonsense made everything better.'

**Please be upstanding for
Her Imperial Highness.**

# DANNY LA RUE

This 'grande dame of drag' used talent, military prowess and a little old-style showgirl extravagance to become one of the most successful drag performers of all time. Daniel Carroll was born in 1927, in Cork, Ireland, and when his father died his mother moved the family to Soho, London. From his bedroom window, 11-year-old Danny could see the glittering lights of the Palace Theatre and vowed someday his name would be up there, too.

The family were evacuated to Devon during WWII, and after a brief stint as a window dresser, he joined the navy and enrolled in the entertainment corps. Drag performances were a surprisingly popular way of entertaining the troops and when the war ended an influx of wannabe drag stars hit London's theatreland – with Danny Carroll the most eager of them all. One of his earliest performances in the capital was Soldiers in Skirts, a bawdy all-male drag review, but in 1954, club promotor and drag artist Ted Gatty thought Danny was ready for his first solo run. His first gig was the comic turn in a seedy strip club under the new name Danny LaRue. In the late 50s, London felt like the centre of the world, and Danny slowly moved to more and more prestigious venues, until he became the star of Soho, headlining shows and even owning his own club.

By his mid-50s, Danny La Rue was a household name, and a national treasure in the UK and Australia, but a dodgy business deal saw him postpone his retirement. He continued to tour extensively, often to dwindling crowds, but finally realised an ambition even greater than seeing his name in lights. In 2002 Danny La Rue was awarded an OBE in the Queen's Birthday Honours List. His legacy is perhaps a theatrical drag style that many contemporary queens have built on, or rebelled against, today.

**A war-time queen,
leaving a legacy of theatrical drag.**

# ALASKA THUNDERFUCK

HIEEEE! Bratish bombshell Alaska Thunderfuck (named after a particularly powerful strain of marijuana) is the young Pennsylvanian upstart whose waspish, extra-terrestrial glamour and sharp one-liners have put her firmly in the spotlight.

Underneath the glitter and snark is Justin Andrew Honard (born 1985), who fell into drag after moving to Los Angeles to become an actor. Alaska is Honard's creation, cut from her on-stage performances at legendary drag night Trannyshack. Although she apparently auditioned for every season of *Drag Race*, it was only season five that producers finally let her show the world just what she can do. She came fifth, but then returned for *All Stars 2* and scooped the top spot. She now tours extensively, and makes *Race Chaser*, a *Drag Race* recap podcast with fellow alumna Willam Belli, but it's her comedic, untucked dance-music albums that are the real brow-raiser. With 2015's *Anus*, 2016's *Poundcake* and 2019's *Vagina*, Alaska has cleverly parlayed into a sort of underground pop diva, with *Anus* scoring the number one dance music album slot in the US on its release. But Alaska hasn't let the fame go to her head and can still invoke the trash aesthetic that made her famous on *Drag Race*: why else would she star in *The Last Sharknado*?

**Extra-terrestrial glamour
and sharp one-liners.**

# SON OF A TUTU

Beloved British drag sensation Son of a Tutu (aka Jide Salami) is the *gele*-wearing, middle-aged African queen who draws her energy from the sun. Her performance style – comedic, heartfelt and ever so slightly wonky – won her first place at *Drag Idol* 2011 and a host of adoring fans. Since then, Tutu's been a busy lady with hosting gigs, fashion collabs and even a role in the movie adaptation of the musical *Everybody's Talking About Jamie*.

Born to an ultra-conservative religious family in London, Jide spent his formative years in Nigeria. As a child, he would wait until his parents had gone to work, sneak into his mother's wardrobe and dress up in her clothes to put on a show for the local kids. Jide remembers his father's anger when he was discovered mid-performance. It took him more than three decades to re-start his dream of being a drag queen.

With one high-heeled foot in Lagos and the other in her hometown, London, there's a delicious tension in Tutu's work. In a country where even basic LGBTQ+ rights are not recognised, many Nigerians believe Jide's cultural heritage is at odds with drag – and being gay. Tutu has other ideas. 'We are as gay as any other country,' Tutu told the BBC in 2018. She is hopeful about the future of LGBTQ+ life in Africa and even has a dream of performing at gay pride in Nigeria one day. Until then, you can find Son of a Tutu performing across the UK and beyond.

There's a delicious tension
in Tutu's work.

# MRS SHUFFLEWICK

Those who know go misty-eyed at the mention of Mrs Shufflewick, the almost-forgotten early 1960s television drag comedy star whose layered, filthy-in-disguise jokes delighted kids and adults alike. The creation of Rex Jameson (born 1924), Mrs Shufflewick was a small, unassuming cockney woman in her favourite pub, getting tipsy on port and lemon, and regaling those who would listen with bawdy stories.

After a simple childhood in a small coastal town, Rex's family moved to London in WWII during the Blitz. Rex went to the local theatre every Monday and saw anything that was on, and later, in the Royal Air Force, he joined a services review show and finally got a taste of performing himself. Returning to the UK, he performed a range of characters, but it was Mrs Shufflewick who won peoples' hearts.

Rex's fame grew but, like most gay entertainers at the time, he kept his sexuality off stage and out of the public eye. He became a cabaret star and appeared on radio and TV, spending more and more time in 'Shuff's' costume, wearing it around London's Soho and to BBC radio records, the two sides of Rex becoming one. Fame saw Shuff bet and booze, he was declared bankrupt but kept working, and his act became a little rougher, with Mrs Shufflewick no longer tipsy but stone-cold drunk.

Homosexuality was decriminalised in the UK in 1967 and, by the early 1970s, Shuff's sexuality was common knowledge. He found a new audience in London's burgeoning gay performance circuit, notably at The Black Cap in London's Camden, and retained his legendary status right up until his death in 1983.

**Mrs Shufflewick won
peoples' hearts.**

# DIVINE

To understand Divine (1945–1988), look no further than the man who unleashed her: cult film-maker John Waters, known affectionately as the 'Pope of Trash'. As the director of low-budget gross-out flicks like *Pink Flamingos* (1972), Waters put Divine in front of the camera and allowed the wonderfully grotesque drag superstar to do her worst – and she did just that.

Divine's creator, Harris Glenn Milstead, spent most of his childhood in Lutherville, Maryland, then a crushingly humdrum and conservative American suburb. Plump and femme, Glenn was bullied at school, finally finding friendship via his neighbour Waters. Together, they created Divine, a big bad girl from the wrong side of the tracks. All bravado and bosoms, the dangerous drag monster first appeared in Waters' 1966 film *Roman Candles* and then *Eat Your Makeup* (1968); Divine helped Glenn reveal a hidden, hawkish talent, hell bent on notoriety.

Through more films and appearances, Waters and Divine's gnarly audience of counterculture freaks and geeks grew into a devoted following, and Divine's star was in the ascendant. Theatre followed, more cinematic work, trash pop music releases, health challenges, debt and then Waters' *Hairspray* (1988) where Divine was convinced to drop her glamour look to play the tragi-comic character Edna Turnblad – to huge acclaim. Through all this, Glenn wished for an acting career of his own, away from Divine, yet successful auditions rarely secured him a role. Finally, in 1988, he achieved his dream: a spot on comedy show *Married... With Children;* only he died of an enlarged heart the night before filming.

Although the infamous scene in *Pink Flamingos* where Divine eats dog poop seems to be Glen's career-defining moment, perhaps we should first remember his jaw-dropping mastery of gender, taste, high camp and a brazen, busty queerness.

**All bravado and bosoms,
a dangerous drag monster.**

# LATRICE ROYALE

Larger than life Latrice is one of the most famous queens from *Drag Race*, known for her level-headedness and wit, and for commanding a feverish fanbase. Straight outta Compton, Latrice's creator Timothy Wilcots (born 1972) first dabbled in drag in the early 90s on American sketch show *In Living Color,* and soon after performed on the club circuit in Fort Lauderdale, Florida where she's lived for more than two decades.

When it comes to *Drag Race*, Latrice is three times a lady. She first appeared on *Drag Race 4* (runner up, but won Miss Congeniality), and runner up again in seasons one and four of *All Stars*. Latrice is one of the many drag queens whose life has been irrevocably changed since appearing on the show. The 'large and in charge, chunky yet funky' drag superstar has a string of commercial clients and tours internationally with her act, and is a talent manager for other acts, but it's not always been easy. As she explains: 'After years in the clubs and paying for some bad choices that led to my incarceration, I was literally forced to re-mould myself into a stronger, more dedicated individual.' So, when Latrice Royale tells you to 'get up, look sickening and make them eat it!' you know she's speaking from the heart.

'Large and in charge,
chunky yet funky.'

# VICTORIA SIN

Sometimes, drag is less about taping up your nether regions and cracking beyond-the-pale jokes in a $1,000 wig and more about performance in its purest form, an art practice with the power and intent to challenge and disrupt. At the centre of this artful new drag is non-binary Canadian artist Victoria Sin (born 1991). Through film, writing, zines, illustration and drag-edged performance, this award-winning new queen on the block has scored themself a loyal following in the contemporary art-drag community (fellow performers Crystal Rasmussen and Amrou Al-Kadhi count themselves as huge fans).

Moving to London in 2009 allowed Sin to explore drag and performance their own way. There were no assigned-female-at-birth drag artists in their native Toronto and Sin liked how, in London, drag is less about passing as a woman, and more about playing around with gender. Sin's own brand of speculative and science fiction underlies their work, exploring its relationship to queer resistance; fantastical stories to take apart the 'processes of desire, identification and objectification.' Their ongoing project *Dream Babes* pulls together these queer San Franciscan ideas with a series of happenings.

Sin's own drag character is inspired by 'icons of femininity': legendary Hollywood stars such as Marilyn Monroe and Jayne Mansfield, cartoon character Jessica Rabbit and legendary female drag performer Holestar. But their character explores and underlines the drag scene's 'subtle but very present misogynist undertone', they told London's *Evening Standard*; 'often the butt of the joke is women. But, for me, the butt of the joke is gender.'

**Performance in its
purest form.**

# CHI CHI LARUE

Chi Chi LaRue is the voluminous-haired fiery alter ego of Larry Paciotti (born 1959), the drag artist, DJ and legendary adult movie director-producer. Growing up gay in small-town northern Minnesota, Larry was at odds with the brash machismo of his conservative mining community, but drag, music (Joan Jett, The Runaways, Elton John) and porn very much dragged him through. Moving to Minneapolis, he formed The Weather Gals, the drag troupe in which he unleashed Chi Chi LaRue to the world, and then moved to Los Angeles to make it big.

LA loved Chi Chi – her acid wit, her more-to-love stature – and she remains something of a legend in the city. Chi Chi performed at night while Larry worked in a small gay porn studio during the day. The porn industry had long been dominated by straight men making straight porn but Larry saw an opening, so he lubed up and got stuck in. He started to direct his own films – often using Chi Chi's name – wresting some of the industry's feverishly spent cash for queer actors and producers. Soon, Chi Chi became the gay adult film queen of the 90s making hundreds of films with performers – gay, straight, bi – lining up to be in her videos.

Alas, the porn scene isn't what it used to be. Less full-length movies are being produced, semi-amateur content and fan sites are taking centre stage, and bareback sex (a no-no in gay porn for years) is making a comeback; but Chi Chi is steadfast to her art form. She still directs, produces and scoops up awards and, alongside DJing and running a store in LA, she's the creative firebrand younger queens are in awe of.

She's the creative firebrand younger
queens are in awe of.

# CRYSTAL LABEIJA

Before *Paris is Burning* (1990), there was another cult drag documentary: *The Queen* (1968). In one memorable scene a black drag pageant contestant – voluminous hair, rhinestone tiara, impossibly gorgeous – misses out on the top spot and, it seems, uses the opportunity to call out the racial prejudice inherent in the competition. A pageant veteran, Crystal LaBeija became the break-out star of the movie, and the scene became a turning point in drag culture. Perhaps in protest, drag artists like LaBeija made sure their talents powered a new, mainly non-white pageant scene: ballroom.

LaBeija died in 1982 and is remembered fondly as the founder of the House of LaBeija (Crystal's protégé, Pepper LaBeija, mentions her in *Paris is Burning*). It was the first drag house for mainly black and Latinx performers – a house which still thrives to this day – and in 2019, LaBeija was inducted on the National LBGTQ+ Wall of Honor at the Stonewall Inn. To follow the career of Crystal LaBeija is to understand queer culture is not immune to racial bias – and that it often takes a strong, loud voice to point it out.

A turning point in
drag culture.

# PABLLO VITTAR

The astonishing Pabllo Vittar (born 1994) is the Latin Grammy-nominated drag-bombshell from Brazil, a glossy singer-songwriter and mega-star whose flawless looks and sizzling performances have made her one of the most exciting performers in the world. Her TV debut in 2014 – a simple, Whitney power-ballad – shot Pabllo to stardom, and she's sparkled brightly in the spotlight ever since.

Music projects with Major Lazer, Diplo, Charli XCX, Sofi Tukker and Anitta have followed, along with some adroitly chosen brand collabs, appearances and magazine profiles. But it's not all been easy. Pabllo, aka Phabullo da Silva, was a queer kid from São Luís, Brazil, bullied for his feminine voice, until his singing career took hold – and then drag changed everything. At the time of writing, it seems the hard-won rights of LGBTQ+ people in Brazil are under attack. Under Jair Bolsonaro, Brazil's opening homophobic President, gay conversion therapy is somehow legal again, and there's a worrying rise in what is thought to be anti-gay murder. And yet, it's against this political and cultural backdrop that, inexplicably, Pabllo has thrived. The South American nation has fallen for this young, gay and very queer drag performer – and so has the rest of the world (9.5+ million Instagram followers, anyone?). For her landmark Multishow Brazilian Music Award TV performance in 2018, a be-winged Pabllo fluttered down to the stage like an avenging angel, and ended the set leading the audience in a chorus of 'Ele não!' ('Not him!'), the chant of Bolsonaro's opposition.

**A glossy singer-songwriter
and mega-star.**

# MICHOU

At the foot of Monmartre, a love egg's throw from the sex emporiums of Pigalle, is legendary drag cabaret Chez Michou. The jewel in the tiara of Paris' cabaret scene for more than 60 years, the club is the creation of an award-winning performer and French national treasure.

The Michou in question, aka Michel Catty, was born in a northern French industrial town in 1931 but moved to the bright lights of Paris in the early 1950s. He settled near Pigalle and worked at a café on rue des Martyrs, eventually taking it over and creating a dinner-dance club with himself as the main attraction. His *transformiste* drag shows were real spectacles, deliciously camp celebrations of the era's most starry performers from Maria Callas to Dalida to a high-kicking Bridget Bardot.

Quite how Michou pivoted from drag performer and cabaret club owner to national treasure says as much about French society as the man himself. Put simply, he is adored; a living reminder of a bygone era of Parisian glamour with Chez Michou a sort of living monument to drag performance. In France, it seems, his life's work could not go unrecognised: in 2005 Jacques Chirac, France's former President, awarded Michou the Legion of Honour. *Félicitations* Michou!

**Deliciously camp celebrations of the era's most starry performers.**

# HOLESTAR

This former British soldier, sex-worker receptionist, dominatrix and proud owner of an MA in Fine Art from one of the world's most prestigious art schools, is a drag queen with a difference. Her award-winning 2014 show, *Sorry I'm a Lady,* details exactly what sets her apart from the majority of other drag performers (the clue's in the title).

Julie Hole is an artist. She joined the army as a teenager (becoming, um, Private Hole) before studying photography, and trying all manner of other creative guises. In 2003, she remembers meeting resistance when she first performed as her drag alter ego, Holestar; critics felt her gender made it impossible to be an authentic drag artist (she asked, 'why not?'), and once she was fired from a job when her off-stage gender was discovered.

Although she still meets the occasional non-believer, Holestar continues to burn brightly, carving out a successful performance career, and is co-founder of feature 'frockumentary' *Dressed as a Girl* (2016) detailing the lives of six performers of the infamous east London alternative drag scene.

Holestar loves to play with gender and is a true firebrand on stage, who is hellbent on reclaiming drag as an artform for everyone. 'Every day I'm incredibly grateful for who I am,' she explains; 'a loud, opinionated, queer, kinky, ridiculous person who has performed all over the world in a wig and just happens to have a vagina.'

**Sorry, I'm a Lady.**

# LINDA SIMPSON

Imagine, if you will, a Marvel-like universe but with incredible drag queens instead of superheroes. Linda Simpson would be one of the originals – a group of scene stalwarts on whom every drag queen thereafter would reference or reject in the journey to find their own persona. Her secret power? Simply being really, really good at drag (and telling awful jokes).

The celebrated Downtown New York City drag performer, aka Leslie Simpson, was raised a minister's son in Gaylord, Minnesota before moving to New York City to study advertising and becoming embroiled in the drag scene. With its normalcy, the name Linda distinguished her from other wildly named performers of the downtown drag gang. The late 1980s became Simpson's heyday with bookings at the Pyramid Club, feverishly excited audiences and upscale appearances; her star was in the ascendant. Her legendary drag zine, *My Comrade*, dealt in queer politics and nightlife celebs, and she hosted a weekly drag night called Channel 69 at the Pyramid Club. Simpson's photo archive of the era (thedragexplosion.com) is a rich resource of spangles and stars from Lady Bunny (page 22), Leigh Bowery, Lady Miss Kier and RuPaul (page 8) to the nearly-forgotten drag performers of the era.

Perhaps it was her gimmick-free persona and perky professionalism that saw Linda's career blossom and bloom; she is still beloved on the New York City circuit – and rightly so. A pure drag original.

**A rich resource of
spangles and stars.**

# CHARLES BUSCH

Award-winning performer and playwright Charles Busch (born 1954) is drag's theatre darling, a lauded actor-writer who approaches drag as stagecraft and is a legend on, off- and 'off-off' Broadway.

Growing up in Manhattan, Busch was painfully shy and yet drawn to performance. Drag became a way to project a confidence he hadn't quite mastered off stage and seemed to help Busch win parts – freeing his creativity in a way 'playing male' couldn't. Busch first performed in drag at Northwestern University in the late 1970s. The experience was life-changing. Busch discovered his theatrical persona – and, as he has written – found drag 'came from a place of profound love and respect, not only for the great actresses of the past but also for the strength and beauty of the women in [his] family.'

Hundreds of performances later in more than 25 self-penned plays, other theatrical productions, film and TV work, Busch is now a stalwart on the performance scene. In recent times he has dabbled in cabaret and has even been known to appear out of drag (albeit in paisley with rhinestone buttons).

Busch makes it look easy but being stage performer *in drag* in the late 70s and 80s was a radical, possibly career-ending move. But Busch won over the audience and carved a unique, TONY-award-nominated career for himself. Perhaps we can see his influence in cabaret queens like Jinkx Monsoon (page 20) and Bianca Del Rio (page 30) (both of whom Busch is a fan) – proof that there is life after drag.

# There is life after drag.

# HINGE & BRACKET

Dr Evadne Hinge and Dame Hilda Bracket were the frightfully endearing upper class English spinsters whose lifelong friendship and love of musical theatre made them stars of stage, radio and TV for more than three decades. The delightful double act – two elderly ladies dripping with pearls and *bon mots* – might seem a touch vanilla compared with the brattish, hyper-realness of contemporary drag but, Hinge & Bracket's seamless double act was a sensation.

The ladies were the creation of George Logan (born 1944) and Patrick Fyffe (born 1942) whose double-act debut at the Edinburgh Festival in 1974 made them overnight stars, winning them their own radio show (which ran for a decade), theatre residencies, minor opera roles and, eventually, their own TV sitcom *Dear Ladies*.

Drawing on their own families' stories from the 1930s, Hinge & Bracket's attention to detail was astounding. Not only were their costumes completely authentic but their between-the-wars references, chit chat and backstory made them women completely out of time. For more than 30 years, Logan and Fyffe were almost always interviewed in character and the much-loved Hinge & Bracket were considered real (or real enough) in the minds of many of their fans – an incredible feat for a drag act of that era.

**Two elderly ladies dripping
with pearls and *bon mots*.**

# PARIS DUPRÉE

Even if you haven't seen *Paris is Burning* (1990), Jennie Livingston's cult documentary (if not, why not?), you'll know something of the queer subculture the film celebrates. The New York City drag balls of the late 1980s have made an everlasting mark on queer and pop culture, from Madonna's *Vogue* to TV show *Pose*, and the thousands of GIFs and memes inspired by Livingston's film itself. No wonder the film-maker was entranced by drag balls: the scene was electrifying, and at the heart of it all – the exuberant gatherings, the outrageous drag houses of queer kids and their elders – was Paris Duprée (1950–2011).

Duprée was one of the 'big five' house mothers on the scene who, along with Angie Xtravaganza, Pepper LaBeija, Dorian Corey (page 14) and Avis Pendavis, created a chosen family of mostly poor, non-white queer kids who would dress up, dance and perform competitively in Harlem. Little is known of Duprée's own background and, although she joined a long line of performers who had attended the Harlem drag balls since the 1920s, there was something unique about Duprée and her fellow mothers. Not least the invention of vogueing, often attributed to Duprée herself. Paris presided over her own House of Duprée, based in Brooklyn, and became known as the 'mothers' mother' (she inspired a series of houses: the House of Ebony, the House of Revlon, the House of Princess). Not all the ballroom families loved Livingston's documentary: some, like Duprée, felt exploited, but others think it had a positive effect. One thing is certain: the world's favourite queer culture documentary wouldn't have been quite the same without her.

There was something unique
about Duprée.

# AMROU AL-KADHI

Writer, performer, drag superstar and 'professional unicorn' Amrou Al-Kadhi (born 1990) is the London-based creative who loves to push audiences to the limit – and they adore them for it. 'Drag kind of feels like a weapon with which to break the rules,' they explain, describing their performance style as acerbic, dangerous and transgressive; '...in drag I have a confidence to say and do the things nobody else dares to.'

Growing up in the Middle East, Al-Kadhi was drawn to femininity: 'I would often try on Mama's clothes without her knowing,' they say, 'she's very conservative, I'd have got into a lot of trouble otherwise.' When Al-Kadhi began their studies at Cambridge University, they took one high-heeled step further. 'I just knew I *needed* to try drag... I rented out an underground crypt and organised a drag night... and the rest is history.' In the decade since that night, Amrou has become a writer-director for film and TV, a journalist and fully fledged drag queen, performing under the name Glamrou.

Amrou's work explores – among many things – Middle Eastern culture, but it wasn't always this way. 'When I initially started drag, I felt like I was escaping my Middle Eastern origins, because of attitudes towards homosexuality in my family – over time, I've re-engaged with my Arab heritage, and found the beauty and magic of it in my costumes and makeup.' Through drag, Amrou takes the audience to dark places, and back again; a transformative, glitter-studded experience. In drag, 'trauma becomes celebration,' they say. '[It's] is a good home to re-frame your own experiences and shed light on them in a new way, and in that sense surprising discoveries about the intersections of identity are in store.'

**A transformative,
glitter-studded experience.**

# MISS DEMEANOR

Art photographer and film-maker Nan Goldin reveals life in the shadows: five decades worth of candid snapshots and 'social portraiture' that document the underbelly of American life. Goldin lived the life of many of her subjects and found herself at the centre of the Bowery drag scene in the late 80s and early 90s. One of her most famous works is *Misty and Jimmy Paulette in a Taxi*, New York City, taken in 1991. In the stark light of day two impossibly gorgeous queens stare serenely into the lens as they zoom through New York City. On the right is Jimmy Paulette – now a makeup artist (page 104) – and on the left is Misty, aka Miss Demeanor, the fierce, blue-haired drag queen who, for a short time, burned bright on the New York City drag scene. She passed away in 2014.

Drag royalty Linda Simpson (page 86), remembers Misty (aka makeup artist Scott Andrew) performing at the Pyramid Club and posing for the cover of Simpson's drag zine *My Comrade*, her fierce look tempered by a calm, quiet countenance. The young drag star lived in the East Village and, in an obituary penned by Simpson for *Art F City*, she reveals the hidden backstory of Goldin's iconic shot. Misty and Jimmy Paulette were on their way to meet Simpson and another drag superstar, Lady Bunny (page 22), to join them on a float for that year's Pride parade. 'We were all creatures of the night,' remembers Simpson, 'and schlepping uptown before noon took monumental effort. Misty and Jimmy Paulette look serene in their photo, but they might have just been half asleep.' They spent the day cruising down Fifth Avenue on a truck in the rain (Simpson's own photos from the day show the slightly damp, spangly carnage that followed); just a few drag superstars showing off and being friends. Misty had left her drag persona behind in recent years but, around the time of her death, had been keen to reconnect. Goldin's shot and Simpson's testimony help us remember Misty, the accidental art-world icon.

**'We were all creatures
of the night.'**

# HUYSUZ VIRJIN

Huysuz Virjin is the blonde bombshell who spilled glamorously over Turkish TV chat show couches for decades until the censors caught up with her. The drag megastar was a beloved guest – or host of her own raucous cabaret-style TV shows – from the 1970s to the mid-2000s and remains one of the country's most recognisable personalities.

Huysuz, aka Seyfi Dursunoğlu (born 1932), worked as a civil servant for 18 years before debuting his drag creation Huysuz Virjin (which translates, roughly, as 'Petulant Virgin') at the Izmir International Fair and then a national talent contest broadcast to millions. Huysuz was a smash hit and Seyfi decided to dedicate his career to his ebullient drag character in 1970. In the years that followed, Huysuz released records, appeared on her own TV variety shows, and enjoyed the kind of celebrity status reserved for a national treasure.

So, how does a drag queen in a supposedly sexually conservative country become so, well, *popular*? Perhaps Huysuz reveals a contradiction in Turkish society, a gap between the authorities' idea of what Turkey should be and the real Turkey, a place where drag, genderbending performance and sassy blonde divas are truly loved. By 2005, the Radio and Television Supreme Board (RTÜK) pressured Turkish TV channels not to allow Seyfi to appear in female clothing and by 2007, he announced he would no longer appear as Huysuz, but rather as himself. For his final appearances on the Turkish version of *So You Think You Can Dance*, Seyfi appeared not in female clothing as the censors had demanded but in unisex garb with Huysuz's blonde wig. In doing so, Seyfi flipped a sparkly manicured middle finger to the censors showing drag's power to subvert, surprise and dissent. Huysuz lives!

**A national treasure.**

# COURTNEY ACT

Courtney Act is the sublime creation of Shane Jelek (born 1982), a Brisbane-born Australian. Inspired by 1994 drag-classic *The Adventures of Priscilla, Queen of the Desert*, Jelek saw his first drag show in Sydney at the tender age of 18. He loved the over-the-top, theatrical style of the performers, but thought he could create a slicker, more stream-lined, more contemporary character himself. He spent two years on the hallowed Sydney drag circuit honing Courtney's look, persona and performance, before winning a Diva Rising Star award in 2002. Courtney achieved a little mainstream fame 2003 as a contestant in the first season of *Australian Idol*, but it was *Drag Race* (season 6; runner up) that showed the rest of the world just what this leggy power-blonde could do.

Courtney is a sort of meta-Britney, a flawless all-singing, all-dancing Nordic goddess with a 100 per cent untucked Australian sense of humour. Jelek has leveraged a rather shrewd career from Courtney's fame: apart from her successful wig line, Wigs by Vanity, much of her focus is outside the traditional drag arena, and outside the US: TV hosting and reality TV mishaps (her skirt slipped off on a live episode of *Celebrity Big Brother* in the UK; she subsequently won) to the fore. An outspoken LGBTQ+ advocate and vegan, Courtney was a contestant on *Dancing with the Stars Australia* (where she danced with a male partner), she's popped up in music videos (her own, and with Little Mix), and chats on her YouTube channel about feminism, HIV/AIDS awareness and being gender-fluid. She's even scored a few scenes in cult soap opera *Neighbours* – a sure-as-shit sign she's on the fast-track to becoming a national – or international – treasure.

**Courtney is a sort of
meta-Britney.**

# DAVE LYNN

As a child, Dave Lynn (born 1958) would sneak into outrageous London drag venue The Black Cap to see his favourite performers take the stage. It was the 1970s and London was in a state of creative rebirth; 'people were coming alive,' explains Dave. He found drag queens fascinating – and more than a little scary – and remembers being lifted onto another man's shoulders to see Hinge & Bracket (page 90) over the crowd.

A friend dared him to enter The Black Cap's talent contest and he did just that; 'I was so naïve,' he says. Dave's mother helped him with his costume ('I had a hip mum'). He wore a Liza Minelli-inspired get up and, to his surprise, he won. He hadn't prepared a drag name and, dazzled by the spotlights, he simply uttered his own and Dave Lynn the drag queen was born. He went on to hone his craft in hostess clubs before returning to the gay scene as a seasoned performer in the UK and Europe. 'Drag queens used to lipsynch, or mime, as we called it,' says Dave, 'but I started talking to the audience, involving them,' and it worked. TV and film appearances followed, and he has never looked back. 'In my day, drag wasn't really a career. You could count the queens who'd made a career out of it on one hand, but it's actually a choice, now – and I'm totally happy about that.'

Drag is a true artform, says Dave, and can be gruelling work, but admits there's something truly self-deprecating about British queens: 'we like to send ourselves up in the UK,' he says. 'People used to say drag was dying,' remembers Dave, 'but it made it through the bad times, through AIDS, and it never died out.' He loves the renewed cultural focus on drag, the attention it gets, how its power to surprise and delight seems never ending. 'All you need is a pub, an afternoon, and something wonderful can happen.'

**Dazzled by the spotlights, he simply uttered his own name.**

# JIMMY PAULETTE

Jimmy Paul is one of the world's most successful hair stylists at the heart of the contemporary fashion industry. His client list is a who's who of big brands and mega-celebs but, in his youth, he was a dazzling New York City drag queen, immortalised in Nan Goldin's 1991 shot *Misty and Jimmy Paulette in a Taxi*, New York City.

Jimmy grew up in a small steel-working town near Pittsburg. His mother worked as a hairdresser and teacher at the local beauty school; perhaps it was fate that Jimmy was inspired to do the same, making a career taming curls and bangs, albeit in his own way. In his teens he discovered a copy of queer rag *The New York Native* in a bookstore in Pittsburg; the cover featured a glamorous New York City drag queen, and Jimmy told the clerk (a young Pulitzer-winner Michael Chabon) that he wanted to move to New York and do the same. He moved there on his 19th birthday, got a job in a nightclub and realised his dream of becoming a face in the Bowery drag scene.

When Jimmy dressed in drag he went all in – a glamorous look with black wig that he first tried out dancing at the Pyramid Club. He loved creating different characters and looks, performed in a few bands and soon started his career as a hair stylist. On the day Nan Goldin took his portrait in the back of a cab with his friend Misty (page 96), he'd been on a drag hiatus, but Lady Bunny (page 22) lured him back to appear on a Pride float. He wore an ash-blonde wig – a 60s look that marked him out from the crowd. Jimmy remembers that day well – a massive parade with a huge ACT UP presence and a distinctly political dimension. In an interview with Svetlana Kitto for *Outhistory. org*, Jimmy said: '...the thing that I love about Nan's pictures is that we're together: in the time of AIDS, we had each other and we were a family... It wasn't about sex, it was about togetherness – going to the Gay Pride parade, having a great time... And having the option to do that in one of the darkest times in gay history.'

'It wasn't about sex, it was about togetherness.'

# SHANGELA LAQUIFA WADLEY

Army brat and one-time cheerleader Darius Pierce was born in Paris, Texas, in 1981 and loved to experiment with drag and choreograph dance routines for friends. Moving to Los Angeles, he had only performed as Shangela – trademark phrase: 'Halleloo' – for five months before appearing on *Drag Race 2*, scraping by in twelfth place. But, there was something about this brash, comedic performer that fans adored. She returned the following year winning sixth place in *Drag Race* 3 and third/fourth place in *All Stars* 3, all the while honing her stagecraft and blistering put-downs.

Post-*Drag Race*, Shangela has turned her fame and work ethic into a rather lucrative business. As an actress, activist, comedian and singer, she's toured extensively, popped up on influential entertainer lists and hosted the GLAAD awards. Then there's the collaboration with Ariana Grande, scored commercial clients such as Orbitz and the FDA, and roles in *Glee, X-Files* and *Community*. Her most memorable turn was in Bradley Cooper and Lady Gaga's *A Star is Born* – Shangela even walked the red carpet (with Jennifer Lewis) on Oscar night for *A Star is Born* – the first drag queen in drag ever to do so. Halleloo to that.

**Halleloo to that.**

# MORE QUEENS WHO CHANGED THE WORLD

Fashion designer by day, glamour-puss by night,

## DAISY PULLER

is the flower-powered London-based drag queen
with insane bespoke outfits, a kitsch countenance
and an eye-poppingly voluminous wig.

Handsome super-talent

## TODRICK HALL

is a drag all-rounder and some say the singer, performer
and TV talent judge has all the charisma, uniqueness, nerve
and talent to one day knock Mama Ru off her throne.

Professional dancer Thomas Fonua, aka

## KWEEN KONG,

is the dangerously handsome and impossibly tall
Pacific indigenous drag superstar based in Sydney,
Australia who deals in love and sassiness.

Gobby London urchin

## BAGA CHIPZ

is the naughty drag artist, who was handpicked for season 1
of *RuPaul's Drag Race UK*, and who is happy to 'flash her
tuppence', as she puts so eloquently.

The British star of season 1 of *RuPaul's Drag Race UK*

# SUM TING WONG,

is the drag queen with Chinese-Vietnamese heritage,
who calls out casual racism with 110% sassiness and the vocal
stylings of Celine Dion.

Award-winning member of drag band The Vixens is

# TIA KOFI

the secretly geeky and leggy performer who brings glamour,
laughs and politics to her set, and holds a torch for *Doctor Who*.

Stylist, photographer and gender-queer artist

# ETCETERA ETCETERA

is the Sydney-based queen whose 'performative activism'
delights drag-lovers across Australia and beyond.

Sweet AF drag confection

# CARA MELLE

is the super-femme, Atlanta-born performer based in London
with the honey-voiced vocals and Beyoncé looks.

Mistress and queen of the surreal and bizarre,
drama school kid and onetime teen goth

# METH

is the London-based drag queen with a 90s club kid
edge. A word of warning: she's addictive.

# ABOUT THE AUTHOR

**Dan Jones is a London-based drag devotee who writes about style, booze, grooming and very queer things.**

# ACKNOWLEDGEMENTS

Thanks to the totally sickening
Will Larnach-Jones, butch queen
Dr Erman Sözüdoğru, body-ody-ody
Liam Calder, 100% fierce illustrator
Michele Rosenthal and designer
Michelle Noel, lil' miss cheesecakes,
Rebecca Fitzsimons and Eila Purvis,
and my dear, dear drag mother,
Glenn Waldron.

Published in 2020 by Hardie Grant Books,
an imprint of Hardie Grant Publishing

Hardie Grant Books (London)
5th & 6th Floors
52–54 Southwark Street
London SE1 1UN

Hardie Grant Books (Melbourne)
Building 1, 658 Church Street
Richmond, Victoria 3121

hardiegrantbooks.com

British Library Cataloguing-in-Publication Data. A catalogue record for this book is
available from the British Library.

50 Drag Queens Who Changed the World
ISBN: 978-1-78488-322-5

10 9 8 7 6 5 4 3 2 1

Publishing Director: Kate Pollard
Editor: Eila Purvis
Designer: Studio Noel
Illustrations: Michele Rosenthal

Colour reproduction by p2d
Printed and bound in China by Leo Paper Products Ltd.